Free Opensource Office Suite Software Apps For Windows 11 OS

by

Cyber Jannah Sakura

2024

Cyber Jannah Sakura

Publishing

2024

Chapter 1 Prologue

A free open-source office suite is a software application that provides a collection of productivity tools, such as word processors, spreadsheets, presentations, and database management systems.

These software applications are typically free to download and use, and they are developed and maintained by communities of developers and contributors worldwide.

They are released under a license that allows users to access, use, modify, and distribute the software's source code freely.

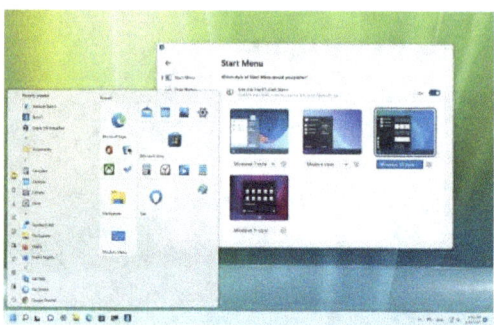

Open-source office suite software applications are typically free to download and use, and they are developed and maintained by communities of developers and contributors worldwide.

These applications are designed to provide users with an alternative to commercial office suite software tools, such as Microsoft Office App or Apple iWork App.

Open-source office suite software applications offer a wide range of features and functionality, such as document creation and editing, formatting and styling, data analysis and management, and presentation design and delivery.

Chapter 2 The History of Windows 11 OS Development

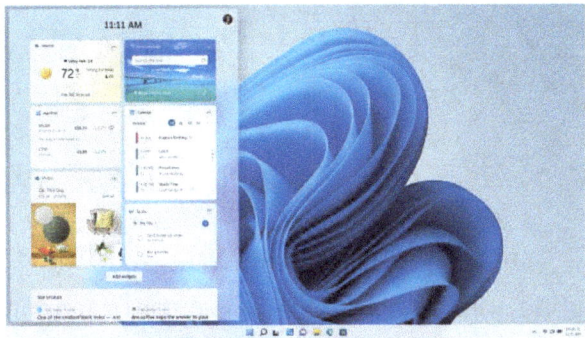

Windows 11 represents a significant milestone in the evolution of Microsoft's operating system, but its journey to fruition was marked by a series of twists and turns.

The development of Windows 11 can be traced back to the aftermath of Windows 10's release in 2015. Despite its success, Windows 10 faced criticism for its user interface inconsistencies and legacy code burden.

Microsoft began exploring options for a more streamlined and modern operating system that could better adapt to the changing landscape of computing.

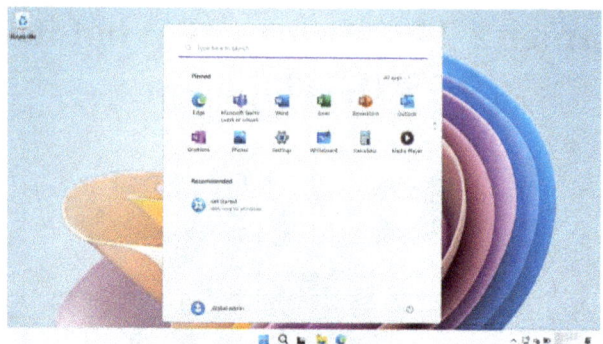

Rumors about a successor to Windows 10 started circulating in 2019 when Microsoft announced "Windows Lite," an alternative lightweight operating system aimed at competing with Chrome OS.

While Windows Lite never materialized as a standalone product, its concepts and ideas laid the groundwork for what would eventually become Windows 11.

In early 2021, leaked screenshots and internal documents suggested that Microsoft was working on a significant overhaul of Windows, codenamed "Sun Valley."

This project aimed to revamp the user interface, improve system performance, and introduce new features to enhance productivity and creativity.

As anticipation built, speculation mounted about whether Sun Valley would be released as Windows 10 version 21H2 or as a separate iteration altogether.

In June 2021, Microsoft officially announced Windows 11 during a virtual event. The unveiling showcased a fresh design language centered around rounded corners, centered taskbar icons, and a redesigned Start menu.

Windows 11 also introduced new productivity features like Snap Layouts, Snap Groups, and virtual desktop improvements to enhance multitasking.

One of the most significant changes was the system requirements overhaul. Windows 11 introduced stricter hardware requirements, including the need for a TPM (Trusted Platform Module) 2.0 chip and compatibility with specific CPUs.

This decision sparked controversy and criticism, as many users with older hardware found themselves unable to upgrade to Windows 11.

Throughout the latter half of 2021, Microsoft focused on refining Windows 11 through a series of Insider Preview builds.

These builds allowed users to test new features, provide feedback, and help Microsoft identify and address bugs and issues.

The Insider Program played a crucial role in shaping the final release of Windows 11, ensuring that it met the needs and expectations of a diverse user base.

Windows 11 was officially released to the public on October 5, 2021. The rollout began gradually, with eligible devices receiving the update via Windows Update.

Microsoft also offered a free upgrade to Windows 11 for eligible Windows 10 users, further incentivizing adoption.

Since its release, Windows 11 has continued to receive updates and improvements through Microsoft's regular servicing cadence.

These updates have introduced new features, addressed security vulnerabilities, and further refined the user experience.

Looking ahead, Windows 11 is poised to play a significant role in Microsoft's ecosystem, powering a wide range of devices from traditional desktops and laptops to tablets and 2-in-1s.

With its modern design, enhanced productivity features, and commitment to innovation, Windows 11 represents the next chapter in Microsoft's ongoing mission to empower individuals and organizations worldwide.

Chapter 3 New Windows 11 OS Superior Feature

Windows 11 brings several superior features that enhance user experience, productivity, and security. Here are 13 notable features:

1. **Redesigned Start Menu**: The Start menu in Windows 11 is centered, providing a cleaner and more modern look compared to its predecessor. It offers quick access to apps, recent files, and recommended content.

2. **Snap Layouts and Snap Groups**: Windows 11 introduces new Snap Layouts and Snap Groups, making it easier to organize and manage multiple windows on the screen. Users can snap windows into pre-defined layouts or create custom arrangements tailored to their workflow.

3. **Virtual Desktops Enhancements**: Virtual desktops in Windows 11 have been improved with new customization options and smoother transitions, allowing users to create separate desktops for different tasks and projects.

4. **Microsoft Teams Integration**: Windows 11 integrates Microsoft Teams directly into the taskbar, making it easy to connect with colleagues, friends, and family through text, voice, and video calls without needing to open a separate app.

5. **New Microsoft Store**: The Microsoft Store in Windows 11 has been redesigned from the ground up, offering a more curated selection of apps, games, and content. It also supports a wider range of app types, including traditional Win32 apps and Progressive Web Apps (PWAs).

6. **Direct Storage Support**: Windows 11 introduces support for DirectStorage, a feature that improves game load times and reduces CPU overhead by enabling faster data access to storage devices that support it, such as NVMe SSDs.

7. **Gaming Enhancements**: Windows 11 includes several gaming enhancements, such as Auto HDR, which automatically adds High Dynamic Range (HDR) to supported games, and DirectStorage, which reduces load times and improves overall gaming performance.

8. **Improved Touch, Pen, and Voice Input**: Windows 11 offers improved support for touch, pen, and voice input, making it easier to interact with devices like 2-in-1 laptops and tablets. The on-screen keyboard and handwriting recognition have also been enhanced for better accuracy and responsiveness.

9. **Enhanced Window Management**: Windows 11 introduces new window management features, including the ability to quickly minimize all windows except the active one by shaking it, and the ability to resize and snap windows more intuitively using touch gestures.

10. **Dynamic Refresh Rate**: Windows 11 introduces support for Dynamic Refresh Rate, which dynamically adjusts the refresh rate of the display based on the content being viewed. This helps improve battery life on laptops and provides smoother visuals when gaming or watching videos.

11. **Widgets**: Windows 11 brings back widgets, providing users with quick access to personalized news, weather, calendar, and other relevant information directly from the taskbar.

12. **Improved Taskbar**: The taskbar in Windows 11 has been redesigned with a more streamlined and customizable layout. Users can now pin apps, files, and websites to the taskbar for easy access, and the system tray has been simplified to reduce clutter.

13. **Enhanced Security Features**: Windows 11 includes several security enhancements, such as improved protection against malware and ransomware, enhanced encryption for sensitive data, and better integration with Microsoft Defender Antivirus and other security tools.

These features, among others, make Windows 11 a compelling upgrade for users seeking a modern, secure, and productive operating system experience.

1) LibreOffice Apps

LibreOffice is a free and open-source office suite that offers a range of applications for word processing, spreadsheets, presentations, databases, vector graphics, and more.

It is compatible with various operating systems and supports Microsoft document formats. The history of LibreOffice can be traced back to StarOffice, which was acquired by Sun Microsystems in 1999. Sun Microsystems released the source code of StarOffice as open-source, leading to the creation of the OpenOffice.org project.

In 2010, due to concerns about the project's governance, a group of developers formed The Document Foundation and forked OpenOffice.org to create LibreOffice. LibreOffice has a strong community of contributors and developers who regularly release updates and improvements.

It is known for its compatibility with Microsoft Office formats and its commitment to document freedom.

Additionally, there are portable versions of LibreOffice available, allowing users to carry the suite and their documents on a USB drive or other portable storage devices.

Link Info:

https://www.libreoffice.org

2) Apache OpenOffice Apps

Apache OpenOffice is a free and open-source office suite that includes word processing, spreadsheet, presentation, drawing, and database programs.

It is developed by the Apache Software Foundation and was originally developed by Sun Microsystems as StarOffice.

Link Info:

https://www.openoffice.org/download/

3) OnlyOffice Apps

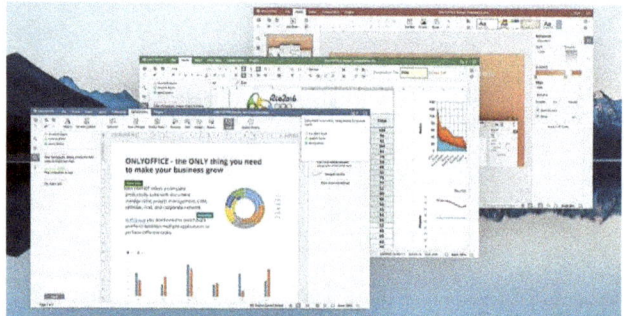

OnlyOffice is a free and open-source office suite that includes word processing, spreadsheet, and presentation programs.

It is developed by Ascensio System SIA and is designed for collaboration, with features like real-time co-authoring and version control. OnlyOffice has been under development since 2009.

Link Info:

https://www.onlyoffice.com/download-desktop.aspx

4) WPS Office Apps

WPS Office, previously known as "WPS" and "KSOffice," has a long history of development in China. It was initially released as Super-WPS in 1988, a word processor for DOS systems.

Over time, it evolved into a comprehensive office suite. The suite supports Microsoft document formats and has a user interface similar to Microsoft Office products.

Link Info:

https://www.wps.com/office-free

5) Calligra Suite Apps

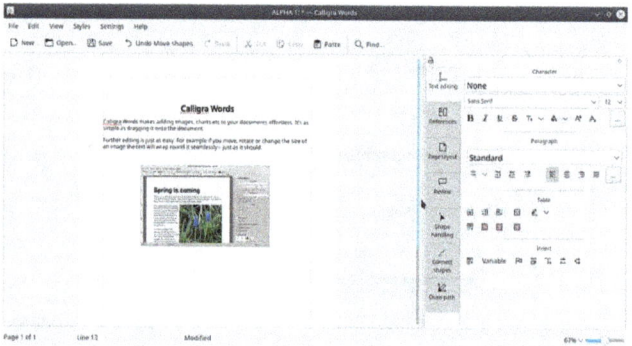

Calligra Suite is an office and graphics suite developed by KDE. It offers a range of applications for word processing, spreadsheets, presentations, vector graphics, and database editing, The development of Calligra Suite began when the KOffice developers moved to the Calligra project in 2010.

Unlike other Calligra applications, Calligra Words was not a continuation of the corresponding KOffice application, KWord. It was largely written from scratch, with a new layout engine announced in May 2011. The first release of Calligra Suite, including Calligra Words, was made available on April 11 2012.

Link Info:

https://calligra.org/download/

6) Softmake FreeOffice Apps

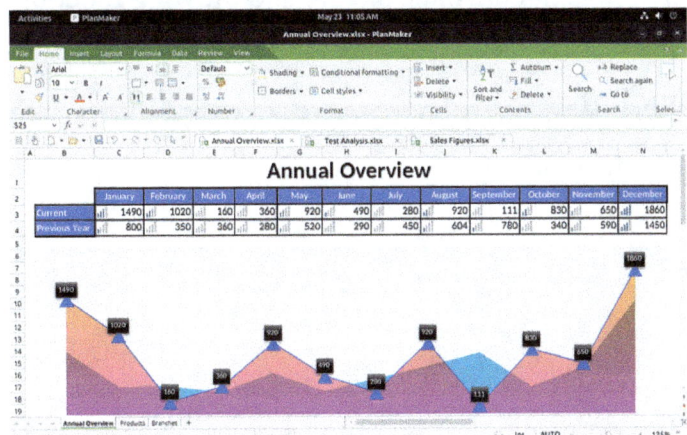

SoftMaker FreeOffice is a free office suite that includes a word processor, spreadsheet application, and presentation program.

It is designed as a free alternative to Microsoft Office and is compatible with Microsoft file formats, such as DOCX, XLSX, and PPTX.

SoftMaker Office, the parent suite of FreeOffice, has been developed since 1987 by SoftMaker Software GmbH, a German company based in Nuremberg.

The word processor in FreeOffice is called TextMaker, which allows users to create documents of any size and save them as compatible DOCX files.

The spreadsheet application is called PlanMaker, offering the ability to create calculation worksheets with various chart types.

The presentation program is called Presentations, providing slide layouts, picture and drawing functions, and real-time preview of formatting changes.

Link Info:

www.freeoffice.com

7) AbiWord Apps

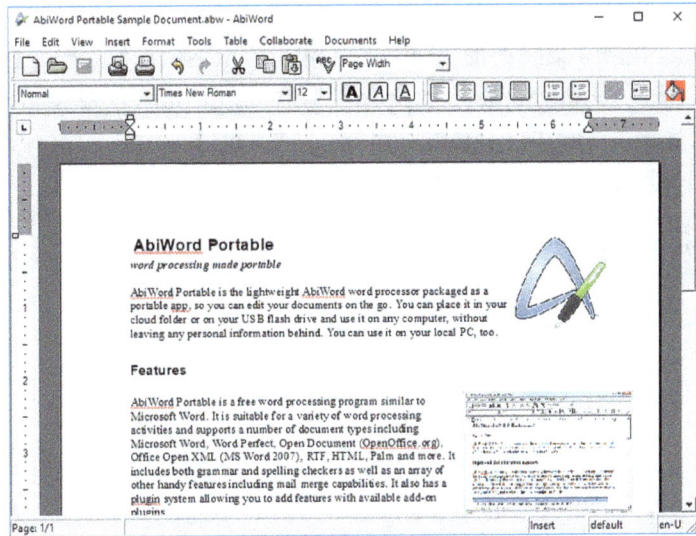

AbiWord is a free and open-source word processing program that is similar to Microsoft Word. It was originally started by SourceGear Corporation as part of a proposed AbiSuite.

Development of AbiWord continued after SourceGear changed their focus to Internet appliances, and it was adopted by open-source developers. The latest version of AbiWord are ver 3.0.1

AbiWord is designed to integrate seamlessly with the operating system it runs on and takes advantage of system functionality, such as image loading and printing capabilities.

AbiWord has received positive reviews for its features and functionality.

Users appreciate its ability to open and save Microsoft Word documents, support for multiple operating systems and major languages, and mail merge capability.

Link Info:

https://github.com/AbiWord

8) IBM Lotus Symphony Apps

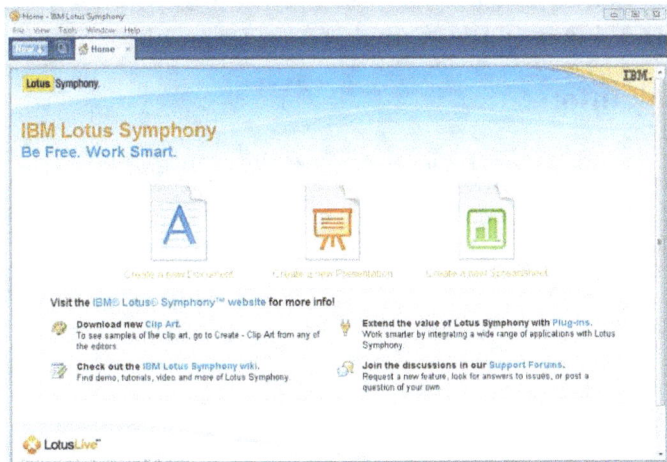

IBM Lotus Symphony is an office suite that includes word processing, spreadsheet, and presentation applications. It was initially released in 2007 as a new office suite based on OpenOffice.org.

However, it is important to note that the original Lotus Symphony was an integrated software package for creating and editing text, spreadsheets, and other documents on MS-DOS operating systems, released by Lotus Development as a follow-on to its popular spreadsheet program, Lotus 1–2–3, from 1984 to 1992).

The modern version of IBM Lotus Symphony, based on OpenOffice.org, offered a convenient, single-windowed interface from which users could launch the three applications: word processor, spreadsheet, and presentations.

IBM Lotus Symphony gained attention as a free alternative to Microsoft Office, offering compatibility with Microsoft file formats and a range of features.

Link Info:

https://www.softpedia.com/get/Office-tools/Office-suites/IBM-Lotus-Symphony.shtml

Author Bio

The Nameless Wandering Cyborg Swordsman from Blue Planet Called Earth

www.ingramcontent.com/pod-product-compliance
Lightning Source LLC
LaVergne TN
LVHW021337080526
838202LV00004B/203